ST PATRICK

Jim Mc Cormack CM

St Patrick: The Real Story
as told in his own words

the columba press

First published in 2008 by
ᴄhe ᴄolumᴃᴚ ᴘʀess
55A Spruce Avenue, Stillorgan Industrial Park,
Blackrock, Co Dublin

Cover by Bill Bolger
Origination by The Columba Press
Printed in Ireland by ColourBooks Ltd, Dublin
Reprinted 2010

ISBN 978-1-85607-607-4

Acknowledgements
Like most translators of Patrick's writings I have worked
from the Latin text re-constructed by Ludwig Bieler. As
well, I have found it helpful to consult other translations,
notably those by R. P. C. Hanson, D. R. Howlett, Joseph
Duffy, Thomas O'Loughlin, Ludwig Bieler and Daniel
Conneely.

Table of Contents

Preface

Patrick lived and died sometime in the 400s AD. He was probably born in Britain, when that country was still a province of the old Roman Empire. After spending six years in Ireland as a slave, he escaped. But he later returned, as a Christian missionary.

Two short documents written by him have come down to us. One of these he refers to as his *Confession*; the other is a *Letter*. Both were written in the Latin language.

They contain the only information about Patrick of which we can be absolutely certain.

The Confession

1/ *Family background*

Patrick's my name.

I'll say it straight: I'm a very plain man;
a sinner if it comes to that.

A lot of people don't think much of me.

I am a Bishop in Ireland.

My grandfather was a minister in the church.

So was my father. He was a deacon, living in a small
town called *Bannavem Taberniae*.[1]

Uprooted

He had a country estate out the road – the very place
I was snatched from. That happened before I was
sixteen years of age.

In fact it was before I had personally come to know
the true God.

Down the years, thousands of our people were
transported to Ireland as prisoners. To tell the truth,
it was no worse than we deserved, for we had no time
for the things of God. We neither kept his laws, nor
paid heed to our priests, who were always on at us
about our salvation.

In the end the Lord, in his exasperation, dispersed us
to the four winds, among a whole scatter of tribes.

Here I am then, a man of little account, surrounded
by foreigners.

---

1. The location of this town in Britain has never been identified.

2/ *Brought to his senses*

It was here that the Lord made me see some sense
about my unbelieving ways. I thought over my past
negligence, and then gave myself heart and soul to
him as my God. Near time, too.

He could see for himself how totally mixed up I was,
and took pity on me in my immaturity. Even before I
really got to know him, or had the wit to tell the
difference between right and wrong, he kept me out
of harm's way; giving me a bit of confidence, and
building up my self-esteem, as only a father can.

3/ *Shout it from the roof-tops*

There's no way then, that I'm going to keep quiet
about this – for what good would that do? I mean
keep quiet about how the Lord favoured me with all
sorts of graces and blessings, in this land where once
I was a slave. For that is how we pay our dues to God
after he has corrected us, and we have taken it to
heart: we show how glad we are by shouting out the
marvellous things he's done, so that every nation
under the sun can hear about them.

4/ *The Creed Patrick was taught* [2]

This is what we were taught:
There is no other God, past, present, or to come,
than the Father who has always been, without
beginning;

2. It was probably the Creed in use in the Christian Church in
Britain and Gaul (roughly, present-day France) at this time.

from whom is all beginning; holding all things together.

And we profess that his Son Jesus Christ along with the Father has most certainly always existed before the world began;

and to have been generated in the Father's Being, before all beginnings, in a way that is beyond our understanding;

and through the Son all things came to be; both what we see, as well as things too deep for our gaze.

He became a human being. And when death had been overthrown, was taken up to the heavens to be with the Father, who gave him all power over everything that can be named on the earth, in the heavens, and in the underworld.

So let every voice confess to the Father that Jesus Christ is Lord and God. We believe in him and look forward to his return in the near future, as judge of the living and of the dead, to deal with everyone as their deeds deserve.

And God lavished the gift of the Spirit on us as the guarantee that we would inherit with Christ, and live forever. For it is this Spirit who forms those who believe and are obedient to God, into his children.

We profess our faith in this One God, of three-fold sacred name.

And we worship him.

5/ *Patrick wants to tell his story, but hesitates*
The Lord tells us through one of the Prophets: 'Call
out to me if you are being oppressed and I will liberate
you; then you will be able to praise me.' While in
another place he tells us that to proclaim the goodness
of God is an honourable thing to do.

6/ So here goes. Despite the fact that I'm far from perfect,
I am going to write this, because I would like my
fellow Christians, as well as all my relatives, to know
the sort of man I am; and to be in no doubt as to
what I have vowed my soul to.

7/ *Nothing but the truth*
I'm well aware that the Lord says in one of the Psalms
that those who tell lies that kill the soul are doomed;
while in the gospel we read that on Judgement Day
every one of us will be called to account for our
careless talk.

8/ So it's with fear and trembling that I should be awaiting
the verdict that's coming to me on that day, when
none of us can go absent or run for cover; and when
every last one of us will have to answer for even our
smallest sins at the court of Christ the Lord.

9/ *Early education*
Actually, for a good while now I have been meaning
to write my story, but have held back for fear of setting
tongues wagging, to no useful purpose.

The fact is, I didn't get the schooling that others [of the clergy] got. They drank their fill of knowledge from the very best that was going, in both Law and Sacred Scripture. As well as that, they did not have to change from the speech of their childhood days, but through steady progress were able to become masters of it.

Having to use a foreign language

Whereas I have had to switch to a foreign language, and you can see the results of that for yourself. You don't have to look too far to see how poorly instructed I am, with no great skill in putting my thoughts together.

Who is the wise man?

Still, a man will be recognised as being wise, not just by the style with which he expresses himself, but also by the depth of his knowledge and understanding, and by the fact that he teaches the truth.

10/ Drawbacks of a poor education

But where's the point in making excuses, even if there's some truth in them? I'd be getting above myself in trying to do something in my old age that I was never able to master when I was younger. It was my sins that prevented me from consolidating the first steps in knowledge that I had taken.[3] Anyway,

---

3. Patrick attributes his capture, and hence his interrupted education, to his sins.

who's going to believe me, even if I keep on repeating what I've said before?

Though the fact of the matter is that I was just a teenager, a tongue-tied lad when I was captured, before I knew what I really wanted, or what I'd be better avoiding. Even to this very day, the prospect of having my limitations put on show for all to see, really mortifies me – brings me out in a cold sweat. For in dealing with well-spoken people, I'm not able to put into words precisely what's going on deep inside me, in the way my whole being longs to do.

11/ *Everyone has a story to tell*

I can tell you, though, that if I'd been given the same chance as the others, I wouldn't have been slow in making the most of it.

It's true that my knowledge is limited and I have to search for the right words. And because of this, some of you out there are of the opinion that I'm getting above myself in putting pen to paper at all. Well, my answer to that is to quote you the scriptures, which say that even those with a stammer can learn quickly enough to come out with words that promote peace.

We are a letter from Jesus

If that's the case, then how much more is it putting it up to us to make the effort, for the scriptures say that we are Christ's 'Letter for Salvation to the ends of the earth'. It mightn't be a stylish letter, written in ink; still and all, it carries the full weight of authority, for it has been etched in your hearts by the Spirit of the living God – the same Spirit who assures us that even the rough and ready come from the hand of the Creator.

12/ God chooses Patrick

So there you have me – the most basic, uneducated rustic; an outsider, uncertain as to what the future holds. But there's one thing I am sure of, and it's this: before I was humbled, I was like a boulder buried deep in the bog. Then he who is powerful came, and in his mercy not only hauled me out, but shouldered me up, and set me on top of the fortifications. Isn't it only right then that I shout out my thanks to the Lord for all his blessings, both those received in this life, as well as those yet to come in eternity – blessings beyond our wildest dreams?

13/ Patrick has a few words for other clergy

So now you God-fearing of every rank, you may well look puzzled; and you, gentlemen, with your clever talk, listen up and explain this if you can: who was it that singled out me, though I was bottom of the class, over the heads of those who seemed to have all the trappings of wisdom: legal experts, powerful speakers – powerful, in fact, in all sorts of ways, and then inspired me, such as I was, rather than others of this stricken world, to proceed faithfully, with reverence and respect to that foreign people[4] to whom the love of Christ directed me.

He told me to look after them – for the rest of my days, if I'm proved worthy; and to serve them sincerely and humbly; and he didn't want to hear a word of complaint from me about this mission.

14/ *His legacy – passing on the faith*

My faith in the Blessed Trinity is so strong that I feel I ought to write this, and not worry about the consequences. Fearless witness to the gift of God's love is called for, with its promises for eternity. If I'm to be faithful, I must spread the name of God wherever I find myself, come what may; so that after I am gone I might leave behind a legacy, both to my brother-clergy and to the children in the Lord whom I baptised – so many thousands of them.

15/ *Amazing grace*

And though I was undeserving, and not the sort of person whom the Lord need take any notice of, being no more than his serving lad, he has been so generous with his grace – and still is, after all my hardships and troubles; after imprisonment; after the passage of many years among this gentile race; such grace I would never have hoped for at any time in my young days. It wouldn't have entered my head.

---

4. The Irish pagans.

16/ *The Holy Spirit takes hold of him*

After I had first come to Ireland[5] it was my daily task
to bring animals to pasture – a job which gave me the
chance to pray a lot. And gradually my love for God,
and reverence for him, got deeper and deeper.
My faith was being strengthened all the time, and
through the Holy Spirit I experienced such lightness of
being, that you could find me at my prayers a hundred
times every day, and nearly as often at night. I did
this even when I was taking cover in the woods and
out on the mountains. Rain, frost or snow – it was all
the same. I was up meditating before daybreak. And I
never felt a bit the worse for it. There was no idleness
in me. I can see the explanation for it all now – the
Holy Spirit had taken a complete hold of me.

17/ *Patrick runs away*

Then one night I heard a voice saying to me in my
sleep: 'You are doing the right thing in fasting: soon
you'll be on your way back to your own country.'
Then a bit later the message was: 'Look, your boat is
waiting.'
In fact it was quite a distance from where I was –
maybe about two hundred miles or so. I had never
been to that part of the country, and didn't know a
soul there. Anyway, I ran away from the man I'd been
six years working for. I went in the power of God,
who led me in the right path every step of the way, so

---

5. i.e. as a prisoner.

that I was afraid of nothing; and at last found that boat.

18/ *The boat to freedom*

By the time I got there, the boat had already been set afloat, and I inquired if they would take me on board, prepared as I was to earn my passage. But the captain wouldn't hear of it, and said to me angrily: 'There's no way you're coming with us.'

That seemed to be that. I turned away from them to head back to the little hut where I had been sheltering, praying as I went along. But before I could finish my prayers, I heard one of the crew shouting loudly after me: 'Quick: these people want you.'

The line must be drawn

So I retraced my steps at once, and was met with the words: 'Come on – we'll take a chance with you. You can prove your good faith towards us any way you like.'

Earlier that day, for fear of God, I had refused to do this by sucking their breasts, as they had wanted.[6] So in the end they came round to my point of view in this matter, and we set sail without further delay. I was hoping, of course, that they would come to believe in Jesus Christ – for they were heathens.

---

6. Apparently this was a pagan way of sealing a contract.

Three days later we reached dry land; then for twenty-
eight days we wandered through a sort of wilderness.
Our food ran out and we found ourselves in the grip
of hunger. It was then that the captain confronted
me: 'So what's the story, Christian? If this God of
yours is all you claim him to be, why don't you pray
for us? Here we are on the verge of starvation, with
little chance of coming across other human beings in
a place like this.'

Put your trust in the Lord
I told him straight that they should turn in faith with
all their heart to the Lord our God, for nothing was
beyond him; and that if they did so, he would put
before them that very day all the food they needed;
for the earth was full of his goodness.
And by the mercy of God, that's what happened. A
herd of pigs crossed our path just in front of us, and
many of these were dispatched then and there.
My companions stopped here for two nights, while
they ate their fill of meat, and thus got their strength
back. For quite a number of them had collapsed, and
were being left for dead at the side of the road.
After this, their gratitude to God knew no bounds,
and I went up a lot in their estimation. From that day
onwards they had food in abundance, even coming
across forest honey. They gave me some, but after one
of them told me it was a sacrificial offering, thank
God I tasted none of it.

20/ *Tempted by Satan*

That same night when I was asleep, Satan grievously tested me. I'll remember this till my dying day. It felt as if a huge boulder had fallen on top of me, so that I couldn't move a muscle. How did it occur to this dunce in the circumstances to call out to Elias? For as I saw the sun arise in the heavens, I began shouting 'Elias! Elias!' at the top of my voice.[7]

Deliverance

The next of it was that the brilliance of his sun wrapped itself around me, and with that, whatever was oppressing me lifted.[8]

I believe it was Christ my Lord who came to my assistance, and that it was his Spirit, not myself, who was already calling out on my behalf at that moment. And I hope that is how it will be on the day of reckoning. As the gospel puts it: 'On that day it is not you who will be speaking, the Lord assures us, but the Spirit of your Father speaking in you.'

22/ He saw to it,[9] that as well as food for the journey, we had fire and dry weather every day until we encountered some other human beings ten days later. As I said before, we were on the road twenty-eight days all

---

7. Christ on the Cross had called out to Elias, the Old Testament Prophet.
8. The words in Greek for 'Elias' (*Helias*) and 'sun' (*Helios*) sound almost the same.
9. I think the narrative makes more sense if the order of paragraphs 22/ and 21/ are reversed.

told, making our way through a wilderness; and by the night we reached civilisation we hadn't a scrap of food left.

21/ *Another escape*

I remember also – many years after this – when I had been taken prisoner, I had a revelation on the first night and heard the words: 'You will be with these men for two months.' That's exactly what happened: on the sixtieth night the Lord freed me from their clutches.

23/ *Patrick's vocation: the call of the Irish*

Eventually, I got back to my family in Britain. That was after a few years. They had a great welcome for me as their son, and implored me fervently never to leave them again, as I had been through so much.
It was there, one night in a dream, that I saw a man called Victor, who seemed to be arriving from Ireland with any number of letters. He handed me one which was headed: 'The Voice of the Irish'. As I read aloud its opening words, I thought I heard at that very moment the accents of those who lived beside the Wood of Virgult, which is near the Western Sea.[10]
With one voice they chanted: 'Holy boy, we are begging you to come and walk among us once again.'
I can tell you it broke my heart. I couldn't read

---

10. Or maybe Voclut or Foclut – probably in present-day Co Mayo.

another word. That was it. Thank God, after many years the Lord answered their plea for help.

24/ *Spiritual experiences*

Another night – God knows whether this happened within me or beside me, for I don't – I heard very learned words which I could not make head nor tail of, except for the last part of the speech which went like this: 'The One who laid down his life for you, is the One who is speaking within you.' And with that I woke up full of joy.

25/ And there was another time that I had a similar experience.

I actually saw him praying within me. It was as if I was inside my body and I heard him above me, that's to say over the inner man, praying fervently and groaning. I was astonished at this, and puzzled, and kept wondering who it could be who was praying within me. Then at the end of the prayer he made it clear that he was the Holy Spirit.

And when I woke up I remembered how St Paul says: 'The Spirit helps us in our weakness at prayer; for we do not know how to pray as we ought; but the Holy Spirit pleads for us with groans too deep for words.' Somewhere else, the scriptures say that the Lord himself pleads in our defence.

26/ *Patrick investigated*

On one occasion I was investigated by some church elders, who turned up with accusations about my sins, that threw all my hard work as a bishop into question. I can tell you I was strongly tempted to despair, then and there, and forever.

But the Lord, true to his name, graciously spared the stranger and exile, and came powerfully to my aid in this humiliation, so that despite the shame of it, and the scandal, I didn't emerge too badly. My prayer to God is that this matter will not be held against them as a sin.

27/ *A sin of his youth*

They came up with something to throw in my face – something that went back thirty years, which I had confessed before I was made a Deacon. My spirit was troubled, and so for peace of mind I confided to my best friend what I had done one day in my boyhood – in one hour in fact – because I was not yet fully in control of myself. God alone knows if I was even fifteen at the time. I was not then a believer in the living God, nor had I been from my childhood, but was still lolling around in the deadness of non-belief – a state of affairs that continued until I was brought sharply to my senses, and really humbled day after day by hunger and deprivation.

28/ Changed for the better

Although I did not go to Ireland of my own free will, and was there pushed to the limits of what I was capable, this turned out to be a blessing in disguise. For as a result, I was purified by the Lord, and so taken in hand by him that nowadays I live my life in a way that once would have seemed beyond me. Here I am labouring for the salvation of others, whereas formerly I hadn't a thought even for my own.

29/ The Lord approves of Patrick

On the night after the day I was censured by the elders mentioned above, I had a dream in which I saw my picture, stamped with their dishonourable accusation. At the same time I heard a voice from God saying to me: 'We have seen the picture of the chosen one, and disapprove of his being slandered in this way.'
It did not say 'you have seen', but 'we have done so', as though in solidarity with me.
As the scripture says : 'Whoever lays a finger on you, touches the apple of my eye.'

30/ Gratitude to God

Because of this, I thank God for standing by me in all of this, and not letting anything get in the way of the journey I had resolved upon, nor the mission to which I had been directed by Christ my Lord. Indeed, I had from God a sense of great personal empowerment, and of having my faith vindicated in the eyes of both God and man.

31/ *A clear conscience*

In all simplicity I can claim that my conscience does not bother me – nor will it in the future. For as God's my witness, there is not a word of a lie in all that I have been telling you.

32/ *Betrayed by his best friend*

I feel sorriest for my dearest friend that he should have been the cause of this unfortunate business. And to think that he was the one to whom I had entrusted the secrets of my soul. In fact, I was told by some of the brothers that before that inquiry – I wasn't there myself, nor even in Britain at the time, nor had I anything to do with it – that my friend was going to speak up for me in my absence. He was the one who had once said to me personally: 'You should to be raised to the rank of bishop' – though I was not worthy.

So what possessed him later on then, to publicly disgrace me in front of everyone, good and bad alike? And that about something for which he had freely and gladly given me absolution, as indeed the Lord himself had – and his is the one that counts.

33/ *The Spirit keeps us safe*

Anyway, that's quite enough about that.

At the same time, it's not right that I hold my tongue when I think of all the blessings God has lavished upon me in the land of my captivity; because it was there that I set about searching for him with real determination; and it was there that I found him.

I believe that it was for the sake of his Spirit living within me, that God steered me away from dangers of every kind, that Spirit who continues to work in me, even up to this present day.

It's a bold claim, right enough: but God understands why I'm making it. If I had only a mere mortal's word for it, I might have kept it to myself for the love of Christ.

34/ *Prayer of thanksgiving*

For this reason I thank my God without fail for keeping me faithful in my time of trial, so that today I can confidently offer him my life in sacrifice – a living victim to Christ my Lord, who got me safely out of all sorts of tight corners.

I can well shout out: Who am I Lord, and what is this vocation you have called me to? You revealed yourself to me as a Being so sublime, that I am constantly praising and glorifying your name wherever my mission takes me among the heathens. This is true not only when things are going well, but also when I really have my back to the wall.

Keeping faithful

I must accept with serenity whatever life brings, and continue being thankful to God. For he taught me never to falter in putting my trust in him. Knowing that he would hear my prayer, I dared to embark on this noble and glorious work – a journey into the unknown, down these last days of the world's history; so that I might imitate, at least in a small way, those missioners whom the Lord once foretold would proclaim his gospel to all the nations before the world would end, to prove to them how much he loved them.[11]

As it was written, so has it been done.

Can't you see? We ourselves are the living proof that the gospel has been preached to the absolute boundaries of human settlement.

35/ *Missionary labours*

It would take too long to go through all my missionary labours, one by one, or even a part of them. But briefly let me mention that the most gracious God often freed me from captivity, and saved me on twelve occasions when my life was in peril, to say nothing of rescuing me from any number of other treacherous situations, too complicated to go into here.

On top of that, God who is my witness, and knows all things even before they happen, used frequently to forewarn me about danger, by means of a divine message, though I was only a poor, simple lad.

---

11. At that time, Ireland was considered to be right at the edge of the inhabited earth – the last country to receive the Christian faith. For this reason, Patrick thought that the end of the world and the Second Coming of Christ would not be long delayed.

36/ *The mystery of it all*

How did I end up with this wisdom I have? It certainly wasn't through any doing on my part. Time was when I hadn't a notion as to what life was about, and God was far from my thoughts. Where then did this gift of knowing and loving God come from?

What a great blessing it has been, even though the price I had to pay for it was emigrating from my own homeland and my own people.

37/ *Looking neither to left nor to right*

People offered me many inducements – sometimes with sobs and tears [to persuade me to stay at home]. But with the Lord steering my course there was no way I was going to give in or be side-tracked. It was no thanks to myself but to the grace of God which achieves the victory in me, that I held my ground in the face of them all, though in doing so I offended them. And not only them, but also, regrettably, some of my superiors.

But my reason was simply that I might come to Ireland to preach the gospel to its peoples: even though this entailed putting up with abuse from unbelievers, hearing myself sneered at for being a foreigner, undergoing various sorts of persecutions – even being put in shackles, as well as giving up my free-born status so that others might benefit.

And if I am found worthy I am prepared to give even my life without hesitation and most gladly for his name.

38/ Indeed, I would like to spend the rest of my days there, if that's what the Lord wants of me.

The wonder of God's grace
I owe everything to the Lord. It was by his grace working through me that many people were born again to God, and soon after that were confirmed. And, new and all as they were to the faith, they had clergy ordained everywhere for their spiritual needs. These were a people chosen by the Lord from the most far-flung regions of the earth – just as he had promised through his prophets: 'The nations will come to you from far-distant lands and will say: How false were the idols our ancestors set up for themselves; they weren't a bit of use to us.'
And in another place, he said: 'I have raised you up as a light for the nations to see, so that you might bring the good news of salvation even to those on the most remote shores of the world.'

39/ *The Good News is for everyone*
And there[12] I hope to remain until his promise is made good – as it surely will be, for he never deceives.
Likewise, his promise in the gospel that peoples will come from the lands of the rising and setting of the sun, and recline with Abraham and Isaac and Jacob [at the great banquet]. Our faith tells us that believers from every corner of the earth will be there.

12. In Ireland

We are duty-bound then to cast our nets with skill and diligence, so that a teeming multitude might be brought ashore to the Lord, and that there might be clergy everywhere to baptise and give hope to a neglected people who were eager [for the word of God]. This was his emphatic instruction to us in the gospel: 'Go to all the nations. Baptise them in the name of the Father and of the Son and of the Holy Spirit. Teach them to observe everything that I have taught you. I myself will always be with you, right until the end of time.'

He also said that we were to bring this gospel to every person throughout the world, without exception; and that whoever believed and was baptised would be saved, but that whoever refused to believe would be condemned.

The last days are coming

It is also written that the end would come after the good news of God's reign had been proclaimed to all the nations worldwide.

Elsewhere in the scriptures the Lord foretells through the Prophet [Joel]: 'In the last days I will pour out my Spirit on all living beings, and your sons and daughters will proclaim God's word; the youngsters shall see visions, and the elderly have their dreams.

In those days my Spirit will take hold of my servants, men and women alike, and they will utter words of prophecy.'

We find much the same in the *Book of Hosea*: 'Those who were not mine, I will call my people, and to one who had not yet obtained mercy, I will be merciful. Instead of it being said of them that they are no people of mine, they will in fact be called children of the living God.'

41/ *The Irish accept Patrick's teaching*

So it has come about that those living in Ireland who had no notion as to who the true God was, and were into idolatry and all sorts of old nonsense, have, not that long ago, been made a people of the Lord, and christened children of God. Even sons and daughters of Irish chieftains are witnessing to Christ as monks and vowed virgins.[13]

42/ *A special convert*

In particular there was an Irish lady, blessed by God. She was one of the nobility, grown to full womanhood, and of exceptional beauty. I had baptised her myself. A few day after her baptism she came back to us with something on her mind. She said that she had had an inspiration from God that she should become a virgin consecrated to Christ, and in this way draw close to the Lord.

---

13. Patrick uses the name 'Scotti' here, which is usually translated as 'Irish'. The Scotti would seem to have lived in the northern half of Ireland, and in what is now Western Scotland.

Dedicated women

Thank God, six days later she gave herself joyfully
and wholeheartedly to God, as the other virgins also
had done – though their fathers would have been
against it. Such women are often subjected to abuse
and ridicule, even from within their own families, for
choosing this way of life; but their number continues
to soar.

Indeed, I don't know how many have been born
[spiritually] in this way[14] through our own ministry,
not to speak of the numbers of widows and others
who have undertaken a life of chastity.

Those who suffer most are the female slaves. They are
continually terrorised and intimidated; but by God's
grace many of them bravely persevere in their chosen
way, despite it being forbidden to them.

43/ Patrick's concern for Christian women

I don't really feel free to abandon women like these,
even to the extent of taking a trip to Britain. I need
hardly say, I would be delighted to see my homeland
and family again. And I would love to visit the
Christian community in Gaul, and meet the Lord's
loved ones there, face to face.

God knows how much I have desired to do that, but I
have been held in check by the Holy Spirit who has
made it clear to me that if I leave my post I will be
held responsible for what happens.

---

14. That is, to a life of consecrated virginity.

The fact is that I am afraid that all the work I have begun will unravel; or rather the work begun by Christ the Lord, who ordered me to come here [to Ireland] and to stay with its people for the rest of my life. With the Lord's help, which keeps me safe from every evil, I will not sin by failing in this matter.

44/ Various trials and difficulties

That's my duty as I see it, though I don't altogether trust myself as long as I am in this mortal flesh. Not a day passes but I find myself grappling with that ruthless opponent [Satan] who is out to undermine my faith, as well as the pure ideals of religion, to which I have made a lifetime commitment for Christ my Lord.

The flesh is weak

The flesh is weak, always luring us to spiritual death through illicit enticements. And I know that, in part, I have not led a life as holy as that of some of the other believers. Still and all, I stand before the Lord without shame, for I tell no lie: from the time of my adolescence when I first came to know him, my love and reverence for God have taken deep root and, so far, through his grace, I have kept the faith.

45/ Don't mind what others think

People can laugh and sneer at me if they like. It'll take more than that to make me hold my tongue regarding the signs and wonders which the Lord revealed to me many years before they happened; for he knows everything, even things beyond time as we experience it.

46/ I should be all the time thanking God, for so often overlooking my foolishness and negligence, and more than once sparing me the weight of his anger. For though I was hand-picked as his helper, I was slow enough on the uptake about what was being revealed to me by the inspirations of the Holy Spirit.

Who does this fellow think he is?
Time out of number the Lord had pity on me, for he saw that my heart was in the right place. The truth is, I did not know what to do about this situation I found myself in, with many people[15] intent on block-ing my mission. They would even gossip about me behind my back, saying: Who does this fellow think he is – putting himself in the firing line among those heathen foreigners?
To be fair, they weren't doing this out of spite, but because my proposed mission made no sense to them – and I can understand where they were coming from, for as I've admitted myself, my education didn't seem to be up to it.

Slow on the up-take
I also have to admit that I was slow to grasp just how much grace was in me at that time. It's only now I

---

15. In Britain

have the wisdom to see clearly what I should have known then.

47/ *Still preaching the same message*

My brother-clergy and servants of God, that's a straightforward account of my story. You trusted me because of the message I first brought you.

And here I am, still preaching the same message, so that your faith might be strengthened. I hope you will go on to even better things. That will be recognition enough for me, for the child who advances on the path to wisdom brings honour to the parent.

48/ *Dealings with the pagans*

You know, as God knows, how since my youth I have lived among you loyally, and true to the faith. And it has been exactly the same when I've been with the pagan tribes. I have been straight with them, and will continue to deal with them honestly. God knows I've never deceived one of them, in anything to do with God or his church. It wouldn't have crossed my mind to stir up trouble for them, or indeed for the rest of us, nor to do anything that would cause the Lord's name to be blasphemed: for the scriptures say: 'God help the man who's to blame for the Lord's name being taken in vain.'

49/ *Danger of being killed with kindness*

Being only too aware of my limitations, I have had to watch myself – even where followers of Christ, virgins of Christ and devout women were concerned. For they were always slipping me little presents, and tossing bits of their jewellery on to the altar as offerings. I insisted that all of these, without exception, be returned to the owners – which didn't please them. But as I hoped for everlasting life, I felt I couldn't be too careful in such matters, in case either myself or my ministry be undermined by charges of malpractice. Nor did I want the pagans to have even the slightest grounds for disparaging or belittling what I was doing.

50/ *Not in it for the money*

Look at the many thousands of people I baptised: did I ever take a cent from one of them? Tell me, and I will give it back to you. Or when the Lord, making use of me despite my unworthiness, ordained clergy everywhere, and I conferred this ministry without charge: did I ever ask one of them for so much as the price of a pair of shoes? Say it to my face, and you can have it back, with interest.

51/ *The back of beyond*

The fact is that I was out of pocket on your account, so that the authorities might let me join you. It was for you that I undertook hazardous journeys all over the country – even to those of you living in the back of beyond, where no one had ever passed through who would baptise, confirm, and ordain clergy. By the grace of God I did all this with a glad heart, for your salvation was the one thing that mattered to me.

52/ *Ambushed*

And all the while I was paying protection money to
local chieftains, as well as seeing to the upkeep of
their sons who used to tour around with me. Despite
this, on one occasion some of them ambushed myself
and my companions, and were hell-bent on finishing
us off there and then, but my time had not yet come.
They stole everything they could lay their hands on,
and chained me in irons. By the mercy of God we
were set free fourteen days later, and our belongings
returned through the power of God and the efforts of
some close friends.

53/ *You're worth every cent*

You know yourselves how much I paid out to those
who administer the law in the various districts I
passed through, on my usual pastoral rounds.
I must have handed over to them at least the price of
fifteen men, simply that you and I might have the
pleasure of one another's company, under God.
Not that I've any regrets about the money I've spent
on you – you're worth every cent of it. And I'll spend
as much again if need be. Indeed, by the end, it's
nothing less than myself that I will have spent for
your salvation. But that's all in the hands of the Lord.

54/ *Not fishing for compliments*

As God's my witness, I'm telling no lie. I'm not looking
for your compliments, nor have I any interest in your
money – that's not why I am writing this. Nor am I

looking to have my praises sung by any of you. It's fine by me if whatever regard you have for me remains hidden in your hearts. We have the promises of the Lord, the faithful One, to sustain us, and they won't be found wanting.

55/ *Who knows what lies ahead?*

Even in this present world I see myself honoured by the Lord, out of all proportion, though it's hardly what I deserve.

I know for a fact that poverty and misfortune would fit me better than wealth and esteem, for Christ the Lord was poor for our sakes.

Anyway, whether I intended it or not, this is the stage I've arrived at – an unfortunate, wretched fellow, without a penny – not that it bothers me.

As for what lies ahead, who knows? Not a day passes but I expect to be slain, or made a fool of, or dragged off into slavery once again, or for something of the like to overtake me. But these things don't scare me, for I have put my trust in the promises of almighty God, to whose care I have abandoned myself. He is Lord of all. As the psalm-writer says: 'Hand your anxieties over to God, and he will look after you.'

56/ *God's ways are not our ways*

Now I commend my soul to God who is absolutely faithful to me. Whatever my shortcomings, I remain his ambassador. For God's ways are not our ways;

that's why he can choose me, from among his least, to be his minister.

57/ *The secret places of the heart*

How can I even begin to repay him for all he has done for me?

What can I say? What can I promise to do for my Lord, when left to myself I can do nothing without his help?

Anyway, he who searches the secret places of the heart well knows that I am ready, and more than willing, to shed my blood for him – as he has let others do who love him.

58/ *Perseverance*

Please God it may never happen that I should lose this people whom he has made his own in this last outpost of the planet.

May the Lord give me the perseverance, for his name's sake, to stand firm as his faithful witness until the day of my death.

59/ *Martyred?*

And if I have ever accomplished anything worthwhile for my God, whom I truly love, my prayer is that he will let me shed my blood for him, as other exiles and captives have done – even if it means I be deprived of burial and, most distressfully, my corpse torn limb from limb by dogs or savage beasts, or left for the vultures to devour.

For I'm certain that even if this should happen to me,
I will still have been saved, body and soul.

We shall rise again
I haven't a doubt in the world that, on the day
appointed, we shall rise up again in the brightness of
the sun; that's to say in the glory of Jesus Christ Our
Redeemer, as children of the living God. Just as Christ
inherited heaven, so shall we. For we will be trans-
formed in such a way that we shall be just like him.
Since it is from him and through him and in him that
we are going to reign.

60/ *Jesus is the true sun*
For this sun which he bids to rise, morning by morning, for our benefit, will never reign, nor will its glory
last. And those sad souls who make it their god, will
come to rue the day.[16]
Christ is the true sun whose glory shall not fade. We
who believe in him, and worship him – in fact anyone who does his will – shall live forever, because
Christ lives forever, reigning with God the Father
Almighty and with the Holy Spirit, as it was in the
beginning, is now and ever shall be. Amen.

61/ *His only reason for returning to Ireland*
Please, just let me explain briefly to you one more
time why I am writing my *Confession*. With a light

16. Some of the ancient Irish seem to have been sun-worshippers.

heart, I want to declare in the presence of God and his holy angels, the simple truth that my only motive in coming back to that foreign nation from whom previously I had such a narrow escape, was to bring the gospel with all its promises.

62/ *It's all due to the grace of God*

And as regards these pages that have been written down in Ireland by Patrick, an uneducated sinner, my request to any believers and God-fearing persons who come across them, and are kind enough to read them, is this:

If what I have accomplished in life has been pleasing to God, in even a slight way, then let no one attribute this to me in my ignorance. On the contrary, let them be in no doubt that it was all simply due to the grace of God.

And this is my *Confession* before I die.[17]

---

17. The last sentence could be translated as: *This is my last Will and Testament before I die.*

A Letter
concerning an attack
on Patrick's Mission

Patrick's mission in Ireland was raided by a British slave-trader called Coroticus, who appears to have been a Christian – at least in name. Patrick, deeply shocked, writes a letter to local Christian communities, some of whom seem to have been supporting this man and his soldiers, who probably had a base in north-eastern Ireland.

1/ *Beyond the Pale*

I, Patrick, a sinner, and in truth a plain man, assert
that I am a bishop, stationed in Ireland. There is no
doubt at all in my mind that this is the Lord's doing.
I'm living here with tribes beyond the pale – an
outsider, in exile for the love of God.
The Lord himself can vouch for this.

Love for the Irish

It gives me no pleasure to give anyone a severe
tongue-lashing, but I'm driven to it on this occasion
by my passion for the things of God. The truth that
Christ has put in my heart has stirred a great affection
inside me for the people and children of this neigh-
bouring land [Ireland]. That's the reason I left my
homeland, and family. I have put my life on the line –
put it at the Lord's disposal, so that I can evangelise
these poor pagans, whatever my unworthiness, and
no matter that I'm held in contempt in some quarters.

2/ *This gang of cut-throats*

I myself have put these words together and written
them down. And I want them brought and handed
over, without fail, to the soldiers of Coroticus. I refuse
to call them my fellow citizens, or fellow citizens of
Roman Christians – fiends out of hell would better
describe them, on account of their foul deeds.
Their whole attitude is aggressive; their business is
death, ganging up as they do with the *Scotti*, *Picts*,
and apostates. Their hands are dripping with the

blood of innocent Christians, an innumerable crowd of whom I brought to a knowledge of the true God, and confirmed in Christ.[18]

3/ *Merciless thugs*

The Christian novices, still vested in their initiation robes, with the sweet-scented oil of chrism on their foreheads, were mercilessly hacked down – run through with the sword by those thugs I have just mentioned.

The day after this happened I dispatched a letter in the care of some clergy, one of whom was a holy priest I'd trained myself since he was a lad, to plead with the gang for the newly-baptised prisoners to be spared, and for some of the stolen goods to be returned. But the soldiers only made right fools of them.

4/ *Spawn of Satan*

I hardly knew who to weep for more: those who were murdered, those who were kidnapped, or those whom the Evil One has tangled up in his damnable web. Those boys are going to end up as prisoners of hell with him forever, for whoever gives himself over to sin will be classified as a son of the devil.

---

18. It isn't quite clear if it was the Picts who were the apostates. If so, the reference must be to the Southern Picts, living in present-day Scotland.

5/ *They've excommunicated themselves*

So let every God-fearing person be in no doubt that I have declared these murderous wreckers of families, these ravenous wolves who have devoured the people of God as though they were scoffing food, to have cut themselves off from myself and from Christ my God, on whose behalf I speak.

The scriptures declare: 'The godless have overthrown your law, O Lord.' This law, though it has been established here in Ireland next to no time ago, has already taken root, and done really well, thanks to the goodness of God.

6/ *They respect neither God nor man*

I don't believe I'm over-stepping the mark in this matter. I have the same authority as all the others who have been called to preach the gospel to the ends of the earth. And to preach it regardless of the opposition – and that includes the opposition of Satan, and his tyrannical agent, Coroticus. That fellow has respect for neither God nor the priests chosen by him; priests on whom he has conferred such sublime divine power that those whom they bind on earth, as far as heaven is concerned are bound as well.

7/ *Have nothing to do with them*

Therefore I beg you most earnestly, who are holy and humble of heart, not to bow and scrape to these men. Don't even eat or drink with them, or accept their hand-outs. Let them first prove their repentance before God through hard penance and salt tears, and set free the baptised servants and handmaids of Christ, for all of whom he was crucified and died.

8/ *Patrick 'throws the Book' at these scoundrels*

It would take too long to go through, or even mention, every text in the scriptures that condemns the sort of naked greed I've been talking about.
[I'll just mention a few of them]:

- The Most High rejects the offerings of the wicked; for to use the goods of the poor as an offering, is like sacrificing a son in front of his father.
- The wealth that the crook has dishonestly stashed away shall be spewed out of his belly; the angel of death will drag him off to be terrorised by the fury of dragons; the viper's fangs will finish him off, and an unquenchable fire consume him.
- Woe to those who bloat themselves with what is not their own.
- Where's the advantage in gaining the whole world, if you lose your very soul in the process?
- Avarice is a deadly sin.
- You must not covet what belongs to your neighbour.
- You must not kill. A murderer cannot be with Christ.
- Whoever hates his brother is, in effect, a murderer.

In the light of all that, how much more guilty is the one who has the blood of God's children on his hands – the blood of those he so recently won for himself, here at the ends of the earth, through my own poor efforts.

10/ *The only reason he came back to Ireland*

As to what brought me back to Ireland: you don't think it was just to please myself that I came, regardless of the Lord's will? What then? The fact is that I am bound by the Spirit of God not to return to my kinsfolk.

Do you imagine it's any credit to myself that I have ended up with such tender feelings for this people who once kidnapped me, and caused total havoc among the servants, both male and female, of my father's house?

I was a free-born citizen, not a slave; my father was a city councillor in the Roman administration. But I traded my free-born status so that others might benefit. I am not ashamed of this and have no regrets about it.

So here I am: a slave in the service of Christ to a remote nation, for the inexpressible glory of everlasting life which is to be found in Christ Jesus Our Lord.

11/ *His own people's suspicions*

And if my own people do not regard my mission as being the real thing, well, so be it. The scriptures confirm that a prophet is never honoured in his own country.

Maybe we don't even belong to the same sheepfold, nor have the same God as our father. Once again let me quote the scriptures : 'He who is not with me is against me, and he who does not gather with me scatters'. For what sense would it make if one man is pulling down what another has built up?

Moved to the depths

I'm not just suiting myself in all this. It's no thanks to me, but to the grace of God, that I am so moved to the depths of my being, and want to be counted among those trackers and fishermen of souls, whom God promised long ago he would take on as missionaries when time began to run out for the world.

12/ *Some people can't stand me*

Lord, what on earth am I going to do? Some people can't stand the sight of me. And look at your flock, plundered and mauled by those slavers I've just been talking about, on the orders of the sinister Coroticus. Any traitor who hands Christians over to the clutches of the *Scotti* and *Picts* is far from the love of God.

Christians had been increasing

Rapacious wolves have gorged themselves on the Lord's flock, which had been increasing marvellously in Ireland as a result of really careful work; so much so, that I couldn't give you a figure for the number of sons and daughters of *Scotti* chieftains who have become Christian monks and virgins.
So don't show any approval for the crimes inflicted on these innocent ones, or their very graves themselves will cry out in protest.[19]

---

19. The meaning of this sentence in the original Latin is exceptionally elusive.

13/ *Stay well clear of those fellows*

The very thought of hobnobbing and carousing with
the likes of those boys, should make any decent
Christian shudder. They have filled their homes with
plunder looted from dead Christians. Armed robbery
is a way of life with them. These wretches don't seem
to understand that they are offering their friends and
children poison for food, any more than Eve under-
stood that she was handing death to her mate. The
same goes for all evil-doers: eternal death is what
they are setting themselves up for.

14/ *Paying a ransom*

It is the custom among the Christians in Roman Gaul
[France] to select capable men who can be trusted,
and send them with large sums of money to ransom
baptised captives from the French and other heathen
peoples. But you would rather murder them, or sell
them to some barbarian tribe that knows nothing of
God. In effect, what you are doing is handing these
Christians over to a brothel. What do you expect
from God for this sort of conduct – you or those who
support or crawl to you? Anyway, God will be the
judge of it. The scriptures say that it's not just those
who do evil, but those who go along with it, that
stand condemned.

15/ *The fate of the prisoners*

Words fail me. I don't know what more I can say
about these poor children of God who have been so

outrageously hacked down. The scriptures tell us to
'weep with those who weep', and that 'if one is in
sorrow, then all are in sorrow.'

This is the reason why the church grieves and laments
for her sons and daughters who, though not yet slain
by the sword, have been seized and carted off to foreign
parts, where sin is blatant – openly so – shamelessly
in your face. Decent men and women are put up for
sale there. Christians are forced into slavery and, to
make matters worse, find themselves slaves of the
lowest and most scurrilous apostates and Picts.

16/ *Patrick cries out to his stricken flock*

Is it any wonder I'm calling out in my heart-broken
grief?

O my most precious and beloved brothers and sisters
and little ones – your numbers beyond counting –
whom I have brought to life in Christ, what can I do
for you now? I fear I am of no help, either to God or
man. The evil of the wicked has prevailed over us. We
have been treated as if we were outcasts. Perhaps they
don't believe that we have received the same baptism
or have one and the same God as Father. The fact
that we are Irish is a disgrace as far as they are concerned. Whereas the scriptures say : 'Don't you all
worship the same God? Then why has each one
turned his back on his neighbour?'

17/ *He's consoled that they've gone to heaven*

On the one hand I'm weighed down with sadness at what has happened to you, my dearest friends, yet at the same time I'm consoled, for it isn't as if I have nothing to show for my work among you: my time of exile here has not been in vain.

For while you have been the victims of the most unspeakably awful crime, at the same time, thanks be to God, you have left this world for paradise, as baptised believers.

I can just see you: you have begun your journey to that place where night shall be no more, nor mourning, nor death; you shall skip for joy, like untethered calves, and you shall trample on the evil-doers, and they will be ashes under your feet.

18/ *Sheep and goats*

Then you shall reign with the apostles, the prophets and the martyrs.

You will take possession of everlasting domains, as Christ himself testifies when he says: 'They shall come from east and west, and take their ease with Abraham and Isaac and Jacob at the great banquet in the heavenly kingdom.'

Left outside at the back door will be curs, dealers in black magic, and murderers. As for liars and perjurers: the place for that lot will be the lake of everlasting fire.

St Paul makes his point well when he says that even the just man will be hard-pushed to be saved; so

where does that leave the sinner, who mocks and
flouts the law of God?

19/ *Sinners blown away*

As for Coroticus and his scoundrels – rebels against
Christ – do they really think they're going to get away
with it, scot free? There they are, dividing out
Christian girls as booty; and all in the cause of a
wretched kingdom that will last no time.
Like a cloud, or smoke that's gone with the wind –
that's how the deceitful sinner will be blown away by
a look from the Lord.
But those who remain faithful will stand their
ground, celebrating with Christ. They will be the
judges of the nations then, and it is they, not wicked
kings, who will rule for ever and ever. Amen.

20/ *We have the Lord's word for it*

I am declaring before God and his angels that everything is going to work out in the way it has been
revealed to me – though I'm only a simple man.
These are not just my own words that I'm setting out
here in Latin, but those of God and of the apostles
and prophets. And they, of course, have never
deceived anyone. Whoever believes, shall be saved;
whoever does not believe shall stand condemned. We
have the Lord's word for it.

Tell it like it is

And I most especially beg any servant of God who volunteers to be a carrier of this letter, to make sure that nothing in it is suppressed or held back, but rather that it be read out in front of all the people, even if Coroticus himself is present.

Maybe they'll come to their senses

And if and when, under the grace of God, these killers of the Lord's people come to their senses and repent of their wickedness even at this late stage, then let them release the Christian women prisoners whom they have seized. In this way they might merit to live with God, and be healed both in this life and for eternity.

I wish you peace, in the Father, Son, and Holy Spirit. Amen.